Notes: (this page intentionally left blank)

E	B	E	O	R	I	E	T	E	M	E	T	H	H	P	I	T	I
1	2	3	4	5	6	7	8	9	10	11	12	13	14	15	16	17	18

DECRYPTION OF THE ZODIAC Z18 CODE

and the "Anti-Z18" Code

First Edition / First Printing

by

Loren L Swearingen

About the front and back covers:

The book cover images are either from the author or the public domain.

DECRYPTION OF THE ZODIAC Z18 CODE and the "Anti-Z18" Code

First Edition / First Printing
Hard Cover Edition

Loren L Swearingen
Author
United States of America

PREFACE / ACKNOWLEDGEMENTS

The scope of this book is limited to the decryption of the Zodiac Z18 messages and also the Zodiac "Anti-Z18" message that is derived from the Zodiac 408 cryptogram.

Due to the unusual contents and nature of this book, the typical layout and structure found in most conventional books are not being utilized.

The precise terminology used by professional cryptologists is also not being employed in this book.

References are listed as they are used in the main body of the book.

The following website was used to help decrypt partial anagram segments: Internet Anagram Server - Wordsmith.org
http://wordsmith.org/anagram/

Licensed copies of Microsoft Office Word and Excel and licensed copies of Adobe Acrobat and Photoshop were used to help generate the contents of this book.

Google was used as an internet research tool for additional historical information.

Notes: (this page intentionally left blank)

What is the Zodiac Z18 Code?

Reference: Wikipedia; Text of Creative Commons Attribution-ShareAlike 3.0; Unported License

On August 1, 1969, three letters prepared by the Zodiac killer were received at the Vallejo Times Herald, the San Francisco Chronicle, and The San Francisco Examiner. Each letter also included one-third of a 408-symbol cryptogram which the killer claimed contained his identity. The killer demanded they be printed on each paper's front page or he would *"cruse [sic] around all weekend killing lone people in the night then move on to kill again, until I end up with a dozen people over the weekend."*

On August 8, 1969, Donald and Bettye Harden of Salinas, California, cracked the 408-symbol cryptogram. It contained a misspelled message in which the killer said he was collecting slaves for the afterlife. The solution to Zodiac's 408-symbol cipher reads as follows:

"I LIKE KILLING PEOPLE BECAUSE IT IS SO MUCH FUN IT IS MORE FUN THAN KILLING WILD GAME IN THE FORREST BECAUSE MAN IS THE MOST DANGEROUE ANAMAL OF ALL TO KILL SOMETHING GIVES ME THE MOST THRILLING EXPERENCE IT IS EVEN BETTER THAN GETTING YOUR ROCKS OFF WITH A GIRL THE BEST PART OF IT IS THAE WHEN I DIE I WILL BE REBORN IN PARADICE AND THEI HAVE KILLED WILL BECOME MY SLAVES I WILL NOT GIVE YOU MY NAME BECAUSE YOU WILL TRY TO SLOI DOWN OR ATOP MY COLLECTIOG OF SLAVES FOR MY AFTERLIFE EBEORIETEMETHHPITI"

The meaning, if any, of the final eighteen deciphered letters (EBEORIETEMETHHPITI) has never been determined with any certainty, though many have tried. These final 18 letters are often called the Zodiac Z18 cipher or code or cryptogram.

ZODIAC 408 CIPHER
WITH LAST 18 CHARACTERS OUTLINED

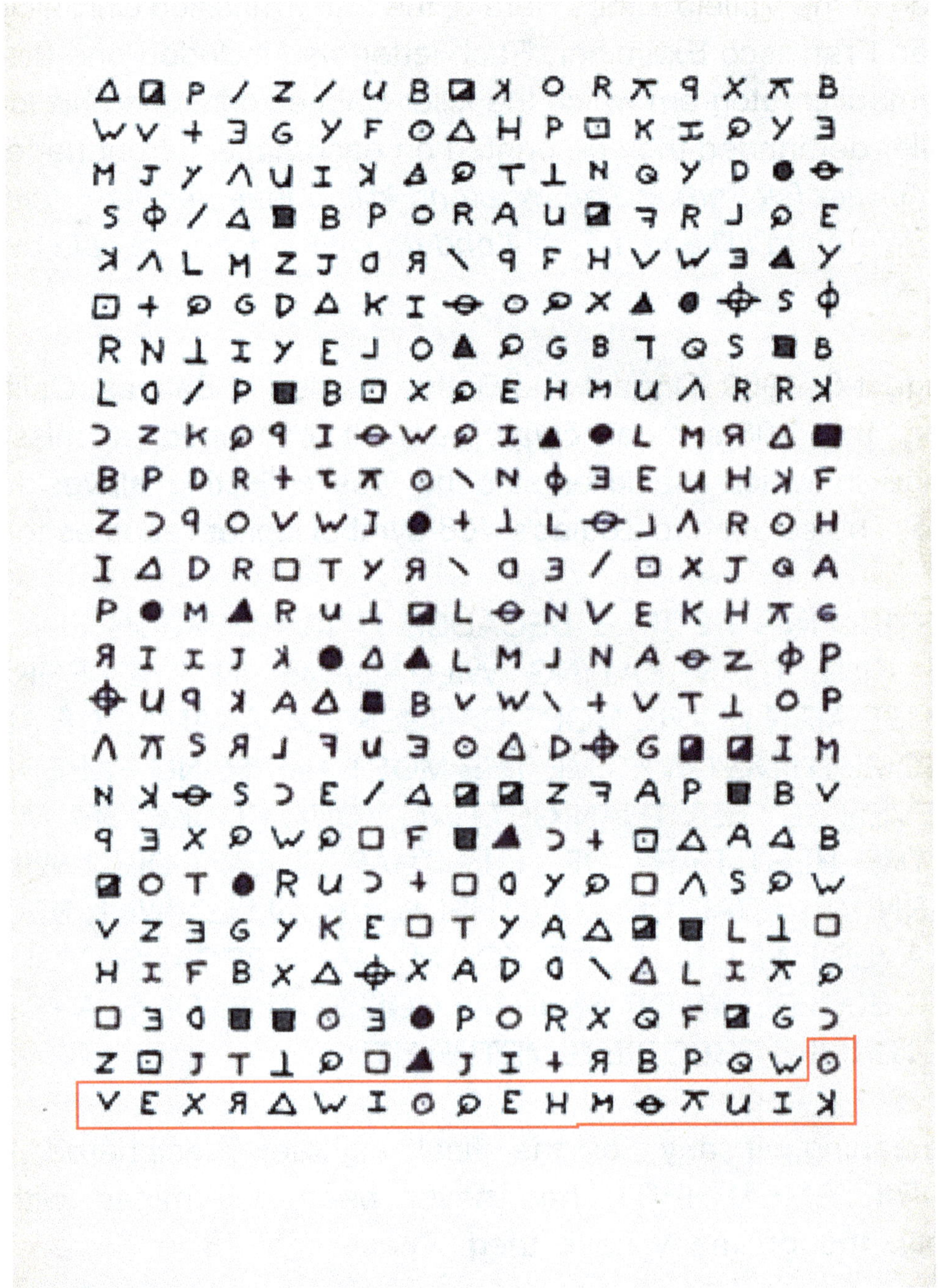

Notes: (this page intentionally left blank)

The Solutions to the Zodiac Z18 Code and also the "Anti-Z18" Code (see attachments)

The meaning, if any, of the final eighteen deciphered letters (EBEORIETEMETHHPITI) has never been determined with any certainty, though many have tried.

The first step in solving the EBEORIETEMETHHPITI puzzle is to link it back to the last 18 characters of the original 408 cryptogram. The next step is to recognize that these two rows of 18 characters represent a linked "double" anagram. That is, both rows of the 18 characters will be re-arranged in a linked manner in order to generate a new decrypted message in the top row and also the bottom row.

LINKED "DOUBLE" ANAGRAM

E	B	E	O	R	I	E	T	E	M	E	T	H	H	P	I	T	I

SOLVED - LINKED "DOUBLE" ANAGRAM (in Latin)

I	A	Q	W	T	O	O	R	U	H	E	X	V	K	I	E	M	O
T	I	M	E	P	E	E	R	I	T	E	O	B	I	T	E	H	H

TRANSLATED TO ENGLISH - LINKED "DOUBLE" ANAGRAM

J	A	CK	W	T	A	R	R	A	N	C	E	VS	C	I	A	Modus Operandi

Jack W Tarrance versus the C.I.A. mode of operation

Time! (Imperative Present Singular)	Perite! (imperative Present Plural)	Obite! (Imperative Present Plural)
Be Afraid!	Perish!	DIE! (fall or to go to meet the afterlife)

There is no "J" in the Latin language, hence, the "J" in "Jack" is spelled here with an "I". The "X" is pronounced as "KS".

It is not an accident that the Latin verb, "morior" ("to die") is not used. The "obire" ("to go to meet the afterlife") verb is more consistent with the Zodiac's afterlife theology.

Note here that two of the Latin verbs, even though misspelled, are still phonetically correct, that is, the misspelled words sound like the correctly spelled Latin verbs. It should also be noted that the English surname "Tarrance" is properly pronounced as "Torrance", which is consistent with the above solution.

The next step is to unlink the double anagram and examine the two single anagrams independently. Here, the last 18 characters of the original Z408 cryptogram are treated as being in the Latin language. The solution below indicates that the person named "Jack W." is giving orders to the "MKUltra" program (see "What is MKUltra?" in the appendices). But what orders is he giving?

NON-LINKED "SINGLE" ANAGRAM

The last 18 characters of the unsolved Z408 code

O V E X Я Δ W I O P E H M ⊖ ⋏ U I Ж

ANAGRAM OF ORIGINAL CODE

I	Δ	X	Ж	W	O	O	H	⊖	M	P	V	E	U	I	⋏	Я	E
J	A	X	K	W		UT			M	Q	U	E	U	L	T	R	E
J	A	C	K	W		"In order to"			MKUltra (dative case)								

Play on words here -- Jack is giving orders to MKUltra

Here -- the theta symbol stands for "T"

The next step is to repeat the previous step and to once again unlink the double anagram and examine the two single anagrams independently. Here, the last 18 characters of the original Z408 cryptogram are again treated as being in the Latin language. The solution below indicates that the person named "Jack W." is stating that he has quit taking medications that are associated with the MKUltra program and that he is doing okay without them.

The last 18 characters of the unsolved Z408 code

⊙ ∨ Ɛ Ж Я ⊿ W I ⊙ ℗ Ɛ H ⋈ ⊖ ⊼ U I Ϟ

Here - the symbol stands for a physical "eye", which translates to an 'I'

ANAGRAM OF ORIGINAL CODE

I	H	⊿	∨	Ɛ	℗	U	I	⊼	Я	Ж	⊙	Ϟ	W	⊙	⊖	⋈	Ɛ
I	H	A	V	E	Q	U	I	T	R	X	O	K	W	I	TH	M	E
I	H	A	V	E	Q	U	I	T	MKU Med	Treatment	O	K	WITH			M	E

Here - RX stands for a medical prescription from the MKUltra program

Again repeating the decryption method above, we now get:

The last 18 characters of the unsolved Z408 code

⊙ ∨ Ɛ Ж Я ⊿ W I ⊙ ℗ Ɛ H ⋈ ⊖ ⊼ U I Ϟ

ADDRESSEES: ANAGRAM OF ORIGINAL CODE

Here - the symbol stands for a physical "eye", which translates to an 'I'

⊙	Я	⊿	Ɛ	⊼	W	H	I	⊖	Ɛ	I	∨	℗	⊙	Ж	⋈	Ϟ	U
I	R	A	E	T	W	H	I	T	E	I	V	Q	I	T	M	K	U
person's name			and		person's last name					I Have		Quit			MkUltra		

Here Jack is telling a person by the name of "Ira" (probably his first name) and "White" (probably his last name) that he has quit the MKUltra program and that they should know about it.

The next step is to again unlink the double anagram and examine the two single anagrams independently. But this time, the last 18 characters of the EBEORIETEMETHHPITI puzzle are treated as being in the English language and is solved by using a crossword version of an anagram. The solutions below indicate that they are three pages of solutions that should be taken as a whole for the proper interpretation of the intended message.

I

B
E
T I P
      E
M O T H E R
      I
      T H E
      E

The second page is depicted below:

I I

H
O
P
B E T T E R
I
M
E

T
H
E
R
E

Here Jack is telling the reader of the decrypted message that he is leaving his present location and traveling to visit his mother, where he hopes he stays for a while.

And the third page is depicted below:

Here Jack is simply telling the reader of the decrypted message to both meet him and Peter at his mother's house or apartment.

Although this concludes the decryption of the Z18 Code, there is also what the author calls the "Anti-Z18" code. The "Anti-Z18 code" is the first, not the last, 18 characters of the unsolved Z408 cryptogram. It is not an anagram, that is, the arrangement of the characters is fixed, but, now read in a different context as depicted in the following:

Here, there are no anagrams

| I | L | I | K | E | K | I | L | L | I | N | G | P | E | O | P | L | E |

"IL" stands for an "internal letter" distributed to an organization or company

| I | L | I | K | E | K | I | L | L | I | N | G | P | E | O | P | L | E |

| Internal Letter | person's name |

So Jack indicates here that he is actually writing an internal letter or memo to an organization, and ironically, the first thing Jack says is that "Ike [a person's name] [is] killing people." This solution to the "Anti-Z18" code is the key to solving the rest of the Z408, which is outside the scope of this book.

Solutions
to the Z18 Code

408 CIPHER SOLUTION (THE VERSIONS DEPEND ON WHICH WORDS YOU CHOOSE TO MISSPELL)

```
I L I K E K I L L I N G P E O P L
E B E C A U S E I T I S S O M U C
H F U N I T I S M O R E F U N T H
A N K I L L I N G W I L D G A M E
I N T H E F O R R E S T B E C A U
S E M A N I S T H E M O S T D A N
G E R O U E A N A M A L O F A L L
T O K I L L S O M E T H I N G G I
V E S M E T H E M O S T T H R I L
L I N G E X P E R E N C E I T I S
E V E N B E T T E R T H A N G E T
T I N G Y O U R R O C K S O F F W
I T H A G I R L T H E B E S T P A
R T O F I T I S T H A E W H E N I
D I E I W I L L B E R E B O R N I
N P A R A D I C E A N D A L L T H
E I H A V E K I L L E D W I L L B
E C O M E M Y S L A V E I W I L L
N O T G I V E Y O U M Y N A M E I
B E C A U S E Y O U W I L L T R Y
T O S L O I D O W N O R S T O P M
Y C O L L E C T I N G O F S L A V
E S F O R M Y A F T E R L I F E E
B E O R I E T E M E T H H P I T I
```

18 LETTER ANAGRAM IN BOLD RED BACKGROUND
TENDS TO BE INDEPENDENT OF MISSPELLED WORDS

In this version of the 408 cipher solution, there are 12 misspelled words

LINKED "DOUBLE" ANAGRAM

408 CIPHER SOLUTION (THE VERSIONS DEPEND ON WHICH WORDS YOU CHOOSE TO MISSPELL)

ALL WORDS
WITH COLORED BACKGROUNDS
IN YELLOW, BLUE OR GREEN
ARE MISSPELLED WORDS

18 LETTER ANAGRAM IN BOLD RED BACKGROUND
TENDS TO BE INDEPENDENT OF MISSPELLED WORDS

In this version of the 408 cipher solution, there are 12 misspelled words

LINKED "DOUBLE" ANAGRAM

LINKED "DOUBLE" ANAGRAM

(letter sequence) E B E O R I E T E M E T H H P I T I

SOLVED - LINKED "DOUBLE" ANAGRAM (in Latin)

(letter sequence) I T I Q W T O O R U H E X V K I E M O

(letter sequence) T I M E P E E R I T E O B I T E H H

TRANSLATED TO ENGLISH - LINKED "DOUBLE" ANAGRAM

Modus	Operandi

Jack W Tarrance versus the C.I.A. mode of operation

J A CK W T A R R A N C E VS C I A

Time! (Imperative Present Singular)	Perite! (imperative Present Plural)	Obite! (Imperative Present Plural)
Be Afraid!	Perish!	DIE! (fall or to go to meet the afterlife)

NON-LINKED "SINGLE" ANAGRAM

The last 18 characters of the unsolved Z408 code

ANAGRAM OF ORIGINAL CODE

J	A	X	K	W	O	O	H	Φ	M	Q	V	E	U	I	R	E
J	A	X	K	W		UT			M	Q	U	E	U	L	T	R	E
J	A	C	K	W	"In order to"			MKUltra (dative case)								

Here -- the theta symbol stands for "T"

Play on words here -- Jack is giving orders to MKUltra

NON-LINKED "SINGLE" ANAGRAM

The last 18 characters of the unsolved Z408 code

Here - the symbol stands for a physical "eye", which translates to an 'I'

ANAGRAM OF ORIGINAL CODE

I	HAVE	QUIT	RX	OK	WO◉ME
I	HAVE	QUIT	R X	O K	W I TH ME
I	HAVE	QUIT	MKU Treat- Med ment	O K	WITH ME

Here - RX stands for a medical prescription from the MKUltra program

NON-LINKED "SINGLE" ANAGRAM

The last 18 characters of the unsolved Z408 code

Ө V E Ꙧ Δ Ꙥ I Ө Ꝗ Ɛ Ħ M Φ K ʋ I ϰ

Here - the symbol stands for a physical "eye", which translates to an "I"

ADDRESSEES: ANAGRAM OF ORIGINAL CODE

Ө Ꙧ Δ	Ɛ Ꝏ	W H I Φ Ɛ	I V Ꝗ Ө X	Ꙥ Ꝗ ϰ Ꙥ
I R A	E T	W H I T E	I V	Q I T	M K U
person's name	and	person's last name	I Have	Quit	MkUltra

CROSSWORD ANAGRAM OF ENGLISH Z18

PAGE 1

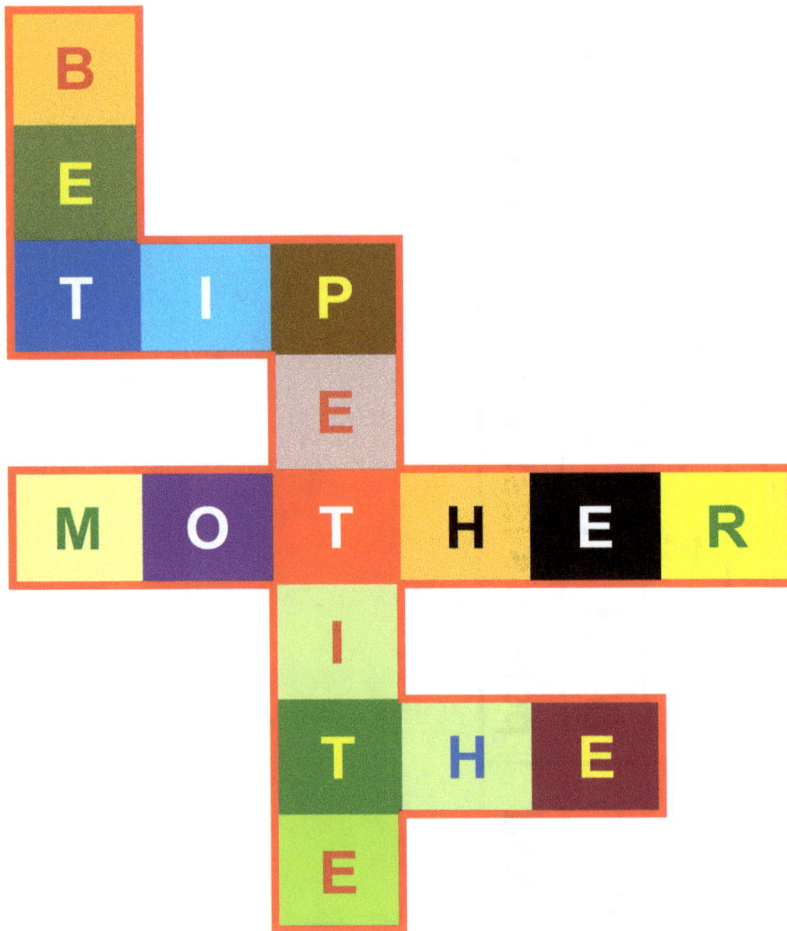

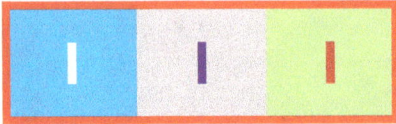

Solution to the "Anti-Z18" Code

THE FIRST 18 CHARACTERS OF THE SOLVED Z408 CODE (THE "ANTI-Z18")

Here, there are no anagrams

I L I K E K I L L I N G P E O P L E

↕

I L I K E K I L L I N G P E O P L E

"IL" stands for an "internal letter" distributed to an organization or company

Internal Letter | person's name

What is MKULTRA?

On September 28, 1984, the U.S. General Accounting Office issued a report which stated that between the years 1940 and 1974, the U.S. Department of Defense and other U.S. national security agencies investigated and studied thousands of human subjects – many who participated involuntarily -- in high-risk tests and experiments involving hazardous substances.

The following is a quote from the study: [1]

Working with the CIA, the Department of Defense gave hallucinogenic drugs to thousands of "volunteer" soldiers in the 1950s and 1960s. In addition to LSD, the Army also tested quinuclidinyl benzilate, a hallucinogen code-named BZ. Many of these tests were conducted under the so-called MKULTRA program, established to counter perceived Soviet and Chinese advances in brainwashing techniques. Between 1953 and 1964, the program consisted of 149 projects involving drug testing and other studies on unwitting human subjects.

[1] Is Military Research Hazardous to Veterans Health? Lessons Spanning Half A Century", part F. HALLUCINOGENS 103rd Congress, 2nd Session-S. Prt. 103-97; Staff Report prepared for the committee on veterans' affairs December 8, 1994 John D. Rockefeller IV, West Virginia, Chairman

Experiments were conducted on U.S. and Canadian citizens in order to develop drugs and procedures that could be used in interrogations and torture in order to weaken the individual and to force their confession through various mind control techniques and methods. The MKUltra program engaged in many illegal activities, including the use of involuntary test subjects. MKUltra used numerous methodologies to manipulate innocent people's mental and psychological states and to alter their brain functions, including the surreptitious administration of drugs like LSD and other mind-altering chemicals. Also used as mind control techniques were hypnosis, sensory deprivation, isolation, verbal and sexual abuse, as well as various forms of torture.

The scope of Project MKUltra was broad in scope, with research and experimentation undertaken at 80 institutions, including 44 colleges and universities, as well as hospitals, prisons, and pharmaceutical companies. The CIA operated through these institutions using front organizations, although sometimes top officials at these institutions were aware of the CIA's involvement. As the US Supreme Court later noted, MKULTRA was concerned with *"the research and development of chemical, biological, and radiological materials capable of employment in clandestine operations to control human behavior."* The program consisted of some 149 subprojects which the CIA contracted out to various universities, research foundations, and similar institutions. At least 80 institutions and 185 private researchers participated. Because the CIA funded MKUltra indirectly, many of the participating individuals were unaware that they were dealing with the CIA.

Project MKUltra was first brought to public attention in 1975 by the Church Committee of the U.S. Congress, and a Gerald Ford commission to investigate CIA activities within the United States. Investigative efforts were hampered by the fact that CIA Director Richard Helms ordered all MKUltra files destroyed in 1973. The Church Committee and Rockefeller Commission investigations relied on the sworn testimony of direct participants and on the relatively small number of documents that survived the destruction order of Richard Helms.

In 1977, a Freedom of Information Act request uncovered a cache of 20,000 documents relating to project MKUltra, which led to Senate hearings later that same year. In July 2001, some surviving information regarding MKUltra was declassified.

Notes: (this page intentionally left blank)

www.ingramcontent.com/pod-product-compliance
Lightning Source LLC
Chambersburg PA
CBHW062022090426
42811CB00005B/924